A seafood recipes cookbook is a compilation of various dishes featuring seafood as the main ingredient. It may include a variety of recipes using different types of seafood such as fish, shrimp, crab, lobster, clams, mussels, and more. The cookbook may also include recipes from different cuisines such as Italian, French, Asian, and Mediterranean, among others.

The cookbook may provide information on how to select and prepare seafood, including tips on how to properly clean and store it. It may also provide cooking techniques such as grilling, poaching, frying, and baking. Additionally, the cookbook may offer ideas for pairing seafood dishes with sides and drinks.

Overall, a seafood recipes cookbook can be a great resource for anyone looking to expand their cooking repertoire and incorporate more seafood into their meals. With a range of dishes and cooking styles, a seafood recipes cookbook can be a valuable tool for both novice and experienced cooks alike.

Garlicky Lemon Baked Tilapia

Ingredients:

4 tilapia fillets
2 cloves of garlic, minced
2 tablespoons of olive oil
2 tablespoons of lemon juice
1/2 teaspoon of salt
1/4 teaspoon of black pepper
1/4 teaspoon of paprika
Lemon slices, for garnish
Fresh parsley, chopped, for garnish

Instructions:

Preheat your oven to 375°F (190°C).
Place the tilapia fillets in a baking dish.
In a small bowl, whisk together the garlic, olive oil, lemon juice, salt, black pepper, and paprika.
Pour the mixture over the tilapia fillets, making sure to coat them evenly.
Top the fillets with a few lemon slices.
Bake the tilapia in the preheated oven for 15-20 minutes, or until the fish flakes easily with a fork.
Garnish with fresh parsley and serve hot.
Enjoy your delicious and healthy Garlicky Lemon Baked Tilapia!

Sheet Pan Shrimp Boil

Ingredients:

1 pound large shrimp, peeled and deveined
1 pound baby potatoes, halved
2 ears of corn, cut into thirds
1 pound smoked sausage, sliced
1/4 cup of olive oil
3 cloves of garlic, minced
1 tablespoon of Old Bay seasoning
1 lemon, cut into wedges
Fresh parsley, chopped, for garnish

Instructions:

Preheat your oven to 400°F (200°C).
In a large bowl, combine the shrimp, baby potatoes, corn, and smoked sausage.
In a small bowl, whisk together the olive oil, minced garlic, and Old Bay seasoning.
Pour the mixture over the shrimp and vegetables, tossing to coat evenly.
Spread the mixture out in a single layer on a large baking sheet.
Roast the sheet pan shrimp boil in the preheated oven for 20-25 minutes, or until the potatoes are tender and the shrimp are pink and cooked through.
Squeeze fresh lemon wedges over the top and garnish with fresh parsley.
Enjoy your delicious and easy Sheet Pan Shrimp Boil!

Honey Garlic Glazed Salmon

Ingredients:

4 salmon fillets
Salt and pepper to taste
3 tablespoons of butter
4 cloves of garlic, minced
1/4 cup of honey
1 tablespoon of soy sauce
1 tablespoon of lemon juice
Lemon wedges and chopped parsley for garnish

Instructions:

Preheat your oven to 400°F (200°C).
Season the salmon fillets with salt and pepper and place them on a baking sheet lined with parchment paper.
In a small saucepan, melt the butter over medium heat.
Add the minced garlic to the melted butter and cook for 1-2 minutes, or until fragrant.\
Add the honey, soy sauce, and lemon juice to the garlic butter mixture and stir to combine.
Pour the honey garlic glaze over the salmon fillets, making sure to coat them evenly.
Bake the salmon in the preheated oven for 12-15 minutes, or until the salmon is cooked through and flakes easily with a fork.
Garnish with lemon wedges and chopped parsley.
Enjoy your delicious and flavorful Honey Garlic Glazed Salmon!

Ahi Poke Bowl

Ingredients:

1 pound sushi-grade ahi tuna, cubed
2 cups cooked brown rice
1 avocado, sliced
1 cucumber, sliced
1 carrot, grated
1/4 cup green onions, thinly sliced
1 tablespoon sesame seeds
1 tablespoon soy sauce
1 tablespoon sesame oil
1 tablespoon rice vinegar
1 teaspoon honey
1 teaspoon grated ginger
1 clove garlic, minced
Sriracha, to taste
Pickled ginger and seaweed salad for garnish

Instructions:

In a large bowl, whisk together the soy sauce, sesame oil, rice vinegar, honey, grated ginger, and minced garlic to make the marinade.
Add the cubed ahi tuna to the marinade and toss to coat evenly. Cover and refrigerate for at least 30 minutes.
To assemble the poke bowl, start with a base of cooked brown rice.
Add the marinated ahi tuna on top of the rice, along with sliced avocado, cucumber, grated carrot, and green onions.
Drizzle some of the remaining marinade over the top and sprinkle with sesame seeds.
Add Sriracha to taste, and garnish with pickled ginger and seaweed salad.
Enjoy your delicious and healthy Ahi Poke Bowl!

Fish Tacos

Ingredients:

1 pound of white fish (such as cod or tilapia), cut into small strips
1/2 cup of all-purpose flour
1/2 teaspoon of cumin
1/2 teaspoon of chili powder
1/2 teaspoon of garlic powder
Salt and pepper to taste
2 tablespoons of vegetable oil
Corn tortillas
Shredded cabbage or lettuce
Sliced avocado
Salsa or pico de gallo
Sour cream
Lime wedges

Instructions:

In a small bowl, whisk together the flour, cumin, chili powder, garlic powder, salt, and pepper.
Dip the fish strips into the flour mixture, coating them evenly.
Heat the vegetable oil in a large skillet over medium-high heat.
Add the coated fish strips to the skillet and cook for 2-3 minutes per side, or until the fish is cooked through and crispy.
Warm the corn tortillas in a separate skillet or in the oven.
To assemble the fish tacos, place a few pieces of cooked fish on each tortilla.
Top with shredded cabbage or lettuce, sliced avocado, salsa or pico de gallo, and a dollop of sour cream.
Squeeze a lime wedge over the top of each taco.
Enjoy your delicious and flavorful Fish Tacos!

Southern-Fried Catfish Katsu

Ingredients:

4 catfish fillets
Salt and pepper to taste
1/2 cup of all-purpose flour
2 eggs, beaten
1 cup of panko bread crumbs
1/4 cup of cornmeal
1/2 teaspoon of cayenne pepper
1/2 teaspoon of garlic powder
Vegetable oil for frying
Tonkatsu sauce for serving
Lemon wedges for serving

Instructions:

Season the catfish fillets with salt and pepper.
Set up a breading station with three shallow bowls: one with the all-purpose flour, one with the beaten eggs, and one with the panko bread crumbs, cornmeal, cayenne pepper, and garlic powder.
Dip each catfish fillet into the flour, shaking off any excess.
Dip the floured catfish fillets into the beaten eggs, making sure to coat them evenly.
Dredge the catfish fillets in the panko mixture, pressing the mixture onto the fish to ensure even coating.
Heat the vegetable oil in a large skillet over medium-high heat.
Fry the catfish fillets in the hot oil for 3-4 minutes per side, or until golden brown and crispy.
Drain the fried catfish fillets on a paper towel-lined plate to remove any excess oil.
Serve the catfish katsu with tonkatsu sauce and lemon wedges on the side.
Enjoy your delicious and unique Southern-Fried Catfish Katsu!

Seafood Gumbo

Ingredients:

1/2 cup of vegetable oil
1/2 cup of all-purpose flour
1 large onion, chopped
1 green bell pepper, chopped
2 celery stalks, chopped
4 garlic cloves, minced
6 cups of seafood or chicken broth
1 bay leaf
1 teaspoon of dried thyme
1 teaspoon of dried oregano
1/2 teaspoon of cayenne pepper
Salt and black pepper to taste
1 pound of Andouille sausage, sliced
1 pound of medium shrimp, peeled and deveined
1 pound of crabmeat, picked clean
2 tablespoons of Worcestershire sauce
2 tablespoons of file powder
Cooked white rice for serving
Chopped green onions for garnish

Instructions:

In a large Dutch oven, heat the vegetable oil over medium-high heat.
Add the flour to the oil and stir constantly until the mixture turns a deep brown color, about 20-25 minutes.
Add the chopped onion, green pepper, celery, and garlic to the roux and cook for 5-7 minutes, or until the vegetables are softened.
Pour in the seafood or chicken broth and stir well to combine.
Add the bay leaf, thyme, oregano, cayenne pepper, salt, and black pepper to the pot.
Bring the mixture to a boil, then reduce the heat and simmer for 30 minutes, stirring occasionally.
Add the sliced Andouille sausage to the pot and cook for 10-15 minutes.
Add the shrimp and crabmeat to the pot and cook for an additional 5-7 minutes, or until the shrimp are pink and cooked through.
Stir in the Worcestershire sauce and file powder.
Remove the bay leaf from the pot.
Serve the seafood gumbo over cooked white rice, garnished with chopped green onions.
Enjoy your delicious Seafood Gumbo!

Seared Ahi Tuna

Ingredients:

2 ahi tuna steaks (about 6-8 oz each)
1 tablespoon of sesame oil
1 tablespoon of soy sauce
1 tablespoon of honey
1 tablespoon of rice vinegar
1 tablespoon of sesame seeds
Salt and black pepper to taste
Vegetable oil for searing

Instructions:

In a small bowl, whisk together the sesame oil, soy sauce, honey, and rice vinegar.
Season the ahi tuna steaks with salt and black pepper on both sides.
Rub the sesame seed mixture all over the tuna steaks, pressing the sesame seeds into the fish.
Heat a tablespoon of vegetable oil in a large skillet over high heat.
When the oil is hot, add the ahi tuna steaks to the skillet.
Sear the tuna steaks for 1-2 minutes on each side, or until browned and caramelized on the outside but still rare in the center.
Remove the seared tuna steaks from the skillet and let them rest for a few minutes.
Slice the tuna steaks thinly against the grain and serve immediately.
You can serve the seared ahi tuna with a side of steamed rice, sautéed vegetables, or a salad. Enjoy your delicious and healthy Seared Ahi Tuna!

Pad Thai

Ingredients:

8 oz of dried flat rice noodles
1/2 pound of chicken breast, sliced (or tofu for a vegetarian option)
1/2 cup of bean sprouts
1/2 cup of sliced green onions
1/4 cup of chopped roasted peanuts
2 cloves of garlic, minced
2 tablespoons of vegetable oil
2 tablespoons of tamarind paste
2 tablespoons of fish sauce (or soy sauce for a vegetarian option)
1 tablespoon of sugar
1 tablespoon of paprika
1/4 teaspoon of red chili flakes
1 egg
1 lime, cut into wedges

Instructions:

Soak the rice noodles in hot water for 15-20 minutes, or until softened.
In a small bowl, mix together the tamarind paste, fish sauce, sugar, paprika, and red chili flakes.
Heat the vegetable oil in a large wok or skillet over medium-high heat.
Add the garlic and chicken to the wok and stir-fry for 3-4 minutes, or until the chicken is cooked through.
Push the chicken to one side of the wok and crack the egg into the other side. Scramble the egg until cooked through.
Add the softened rice noodles, bean sprouts, green onions, and chopped peanuts to the wok.
Pour the tamarind mixture over the noodles and stir-fry for 2-3 minutes, or until the noodles are evenly coated and everything is heated through.
Serve the Pad Thai immediately, garnished with additional chopped peanuts, green onions, and lime wedges.
Enjoy your delicious and flavorful Pad Thai!

Salmon Burgers

Ingredients:

1 pound of skinless salmon fillet
1/2 cup of panko bread crumbs
1/4 cup of chopped green onions
2 tablespoons of chopped fresh parsley
1 tablespoon of Dijon mustard
1 egg
1 teaspoon of lemon zest
Salt and black pepper to taste
4 burger buns
Lettuce, tomato slices, and mayonnaise (optional)

Instructions:

Preheat the oven to 375°F.
Cut the salmon into small pieces and put them in a food processor. Pulse until the salmon is coarsely chopped, but not pureed.
In a large bowl, mix together the chopped salmon, bread crumbs, green onions, parsley, Dijon mustard, egg, lemon zest, salt, and pepper.
Divide the salmon mixture into four equal portions and shape each portion into a patty.
Heat a tablespoon of vegetable oil in a large skillet over medium-high heat.
Add the salmon patties to the skillet and cook for 3-4 minutes on each side, or until browned and cooked through.
Transfer the cooked salmon patties to a baking sheet and bake in the oven for 5-7 minutes, or until fully cooked.
Toast the burger buns in the oven or on a grill.
Assemble the burgers by placing a salmon patty on a toasted bun and topping with lettuce, tomato slices, and mayonnaise (if desired).
Enjoy your delicious and healthy Salmon Burgers!

Lemon Garlic Shrimp

Ingredients:

1 pound of large shrimp, peeled and deveined
3 cloves of garlic, minced
2 tablespoons of olive oil
1/4 cup of dry white wine
1/4 cup of chicken broth
Juice of 1 lemon
2 tablespoons of butter
Salt and black pepper to taste
Chopped fresh parsley for garnish

Instructions:

Heat the olive oil in a large skillet over medium-high heat.
Add the minced garlic and cook for 1-2 minutes, or until fragrant.
Add the shrimp to the skillet and cook for 2-3 minutes on each side, or until pink and cooked through. Remove the shrimp from the skillet and set aside.
Deglaze the skillet with the white wine and chicken broth, scraping up any brown bits from the bottom of the pan.
Add the lemon juice to the skillet and bring the mixture to a simmer.
Add the butter to the skillet and stir until melted and well combined.
Return the shrimp to the skillet and toss with the lemon garlic sauce.
Season with salt and black pepper to taste.
Garnish with chopped fresh parsley and serve immediately.
Enjoy your delicious and flavorful Lemon Garlic Shrimp!

Tuna Melt

Ingredients:

2 cans of tuna, drained
1/4 cup of mayonnaise
2 tablespoons of chopped red onion
1 tablespoon of chopped fresh parsley
1 tablespoon of lemon juice
Salt and black pepper to taste
4 slices of bread
2 tablespoons of butter
4 slices of cheddar cheese
Sliced tomato (optional)

Instructions:

In a medium bowl, mix together the tuna, mayonnaise, chopped red onion, chopped parsley, lemon juice, salt, and black pepper.
Heat a skillet over medium heat.
Butter one side of each slice of bread.
Place two slices of bread, butter side down, in the skillet.
Divide the tuna mixture evenly between the two slices of bread.
Add a slice of cheddar cheese on top of the tuna mixture on each slice of bread.
If desired, add sliced tomato on top of the cheese.
Place the remaining two slices of bread on top, butter side up.
Cook the sandwich for 2-3 minutes on each side, or until the bread is toasted and the cheese is melted.
Serve hot and enjoy your delicious Tuna Melt sandwich!
Note: You can also add other toppings, such as sliced avocado or pickles, to your Tuna Melt sandwich for added flavor.

Salmon Patties

Ingredients:

1 pound of skinless salmon fillet
1/4 cup of finely chopped onion
1/4 cup of finely chopped celery
2 tablespoons of mayonnaise
2 tablespoons of Dijon mustard
1 tablespoon of lemon juice
1 teaspoon of Old Bay seasoning
Salt and black pepper to taste
1/2 cup of panko bread crumbs
1/4 cup of chopped fresh parsley
2 tablespoons of olive oil

Instructions:

Cut the salmon into small pieces and put them in a food processor. Pulse until the salmon is coarsely chopped, but not pureed.
In a large bowl, mix together the chopped salmon, chopped onion, chopped celery, mayonnaise, Dijon mustard, lemon juice, Old Bay seasoning, salt, and black pepper.
Add the panko bread crumbs and chopped fresh parsley to the salmon mixture and stir to combine.
Divide the salmon mixture into 8 equal portions and shape each portion into a patty.
Heat the olive oil in a large skillet over medium-high heat.
Add the salmon patties to the skillet and cook for 3-4 minutes on each side, or until browned and cooked through.
Serve hot and enjoy your delicious and flavorful Salmon Patties!
Note: You can also serve the salmon patties with tartar sauce or remoulade sauce for added flavor.

Mahi Mahi Tacos

Ingredients:

1 pound Mahi Mahi fillets, skin removed
Salt and black pepper to taste
1 tablespoon of olive oil
8 small corn tortillas
1/2 cup of diced red onion
1/2 cup of diced tomato
1/4 cup of chopped fresh cilantro
1 jalapeno pepper, seeded and minced
1 lime, cut into wedges

For the marinade:

1/4 cup of lime juice
2 tablespoons of olive oil
2 garlic cloves, minced
1 teaspoon of ground cumin
1 teaspoon of chili powder
Salt and black pepper to taste

Instructions:

In a small bowl, whisk together the lime juice, olive oil, minced garlic, ground cumin, chili powder, salt, and black pepper.
Cut the Mahi Mahi fillets into 1-inch pieces and place them in a shallow dish.
Pour the marinade over the fish, cover, and refrigerate for 30 minutes.
Preheat the oven to 350°F.
Heat the olive oil in a large skillet over medium-high heat.
Remove the fish from the marinade and discard the remaining marinade.
Season the fish with salt and black pepper and cook for 2-3 minutes on each side, or until browned and cooked through.
Warm the tortillas in the oven for 5 minutes.
Assemble the tacos by placing the Mahi Mahi pieces on each tortilla.
Top the tacos with diced red onion, diced tomato, chopped fresh cilantro, and minced jalapeno pepper.
Serve with lime wedges on the side and enjoy your delicious Mahi Mahi Tacos!
Note: You can also serve the tacos with avocado slices, sour cream, or your favorite hot sauce.

Green Chili Manhattan Chowder

Ingredients:

2 tablespoons of unsalted butter
1 onion, diced
2 garlic cloves, minced
2 celery stalks, diced
1 red bell pepper, diced
1 green bell pepper, diced
1 jalapeno pepper, seeded and diced
2 teaspoons of ground cumin
1 teaspoon of chili powder
2 cups of chicken broth
1 (28-ounce) can of diced tomatoes
2 cups of frozen corn
1 (4-ounce) can of diced green chilies
1 pound of peeled and deveined medium shrimp
Salt and black pepper to taste
1/4 cup of chopped fresh cilantro
Lime wedges, for serving

Instructions:

Melt the butter in a large pot over medium heat.
Add the diced onion, minced garlic, diced celery, diced red bell pepper, diced green bell pepper, and seeded and diced jalapeno pepper to the pot.
Cook for 10-12 minutes, or until the vegetables are softened.
Add the ground cumin and chili powder to the pot and cook for 1-2 minutes, or until fragrant.
Add the chicken broth, diced tomatoes, frozen corn, and diced green chilies to the pot and bring to a boil.
Reduce the heat to low and simmer for 20-25 minutes, or until the vegetables are tender.
Add the peeled and deveined shrimp to the pot and cook for 5-7 minutes, or until the shrimp are pink and cooked through.
Season the chowder with salt and black pepper to taste.
Serve the Green Chili Manhattan Chowder hot, garnished with chopped fresh cilantro and lime wedges on the side.
Enjoy your delicious and flavorful chowder!

Baked Cod

Ingredients:

4 cod fillets
Salt and black pepper to taste
1/4 cup of olive oil
1/4 cup of lemon juice
1 tablespoon of Dijon mustard
2 garlic cloves, minced
2 tablespoons of chopped fresh parsle

Instructions:

Preheat the oven to 375°F.
Pat the cod fillets dry with paper towels and season them with salt and black pepper to taste.
In a small bowl, whisk together the olive oil, lemon juice, Dijon mustard, minced garlic, and chopped fresh parsley.
Place the cod fillets in a baking dish and pour the marinade over them.
Bake the cod in the oven for 15-20 minutes, or until the fish is cooked through and flakes easily with a fork.
Serve the Baked Cod hot, garnished with extra chopped fresh parsley if desired.
Note: You can also add sliced lemon or other herbs to the marinade for extra flavor. Enjoy your delicious and healthy Baked Cod!

Smoked Salmon Pasta

Ingredients:

12 ounces of linguine or spaghetti
4 tablespoons of unsalted butter
1/2 cup of heavy cream
1/2 cup of grated Parmesan cheese
4 ounces of smoked salmon, thinly sliced
1/4 cup of chopped fresh parsley
Salt and black pepper to taste

Instructions:

Cook the pasta according to the package instructions until al dente.
While the pasta is cooking, melt the butter in a large skillet over medium heat.
Add the heavy cream to the skillet and bring to a simmer.
Add the grated Parmesan cheese to the skillet and stir until melted and smooth.
Add the sliced smoked salmon to the skillet and stir gently to coat with the sauce.
When the pasta is cooked, drain it and add it to the skillet with the sauce.
Toss the pasta with the sauce and smoked salmon until well coated.
Add the chopped fresh parsley to the skillet and stir to combine.
Season the Smoked Salmon Pasta with salt and black pepper to taste.
Serve the pasta hot, garnished with extra chopped fresh parsley if desired.
Enjoy your delicious and creamy Smoked Salmon Pasta!

Tuscan Butter Shrimp

Ingredients:

1 pound of large shrimp, peeled and deveined
Salt and black pepper to taste
2 tablespoons of olive oil
4 tablespoons of unsalted butter
3 cloves of garlic, minced
1/2 cup of sun-dried tomatoes, chopped
1/2 cup of chicken broth
1/2 cup of heavy cream
1/4 cup of grated Parmesan cheese
1 tablespoon of chopped fresh parsley

Instructions:

Season the shrimp with salt and black pepper to taste.
Heat the olive oil in a large skillet over medium-high heat.
Add the shrimp to the skillet and cook for 2-3 minutes per side, until pink and cooked through. Remove the shrimp from the skillet and set aside.
Reduce the heat to medium and add the butter to the skillet. Once melted, add the minced garlic and cook for 1-2 minutes, until fragrant.
Add the chopped sun-dried tomatoes to the skillet and cook for 2-3 minutes, until softened.
Add the chicken broth to the skillet and stir to combine.
Add the heavy cream to the skillet and stir until the sauce is smooth.
Add the grated Parmesan cheese to the skillet and stir until melted and combined.
Add the cooked shrimp back to the skillet and toss to coat with the sauce.
Sprinkle the chopped fresh parsley over the Tuscan Butter Shrimp.
Serve the shrimp hot, garnished with extra chopped fresh parsley if desired.
Enjoy your delicious and creamy Tuscan Butter Shrimp!

Grilled Halibut

Ingredients:

4 halibut fillets, skin removed
1/4 cup of olive oil
2 tablespoons of lemon juice
2 cloves of garlic, minced
1 tablespoon of chopped fresh parsley
1/2 teaspoon of salt
1/4 teaspoon of black pepper

Instructions:

Preheat your grill to medium-high heat.
In a small bowl, whisk together the olive oil, lemon juice, minced garlic, chopped fresh parsley, salt, and black pepper.
Brush the halibut fillets with the marinade on both sides.
Place the halibut fillets on the grill and cook for 3-4 minutes per side, until cooked through and opaque.
Remove the halibut fillets from the grill and serve hot.
Garnish the grilled halibut with extra chopped fresh parsley if desired.
Enjoy your delicious and flavorful Grilled Halibut!

Crab Cakes

Ingredients:

1 pound of lump crab meat
1/2 cup of panko breadcrumbs
1/4 cup of mayonnaise
2 tablespoons of Dijon mustard
2 tablespoons of chopped fresh parsley
1 tablespoon of Old Bay seasoning
1/4 teaspoon of salt
1/4 teaspoon of black pepper
1 egg, beaten
2 tablespoons of unsalted butter
Lemon wedges, for serving

Instructions:

In a large bowl, combine the lump crab meat, panko breadcrumbs, mayonnaise, Dijon mustard, chopped fresh parsley, Old Bay seasoning, salt, black pepper, and beaten egg. Mix gently until well combined.
Form the crab mixture into 8-10 equal-sized patties.
Heat the butter in a large skillet over medium-high heat.
Add the crab cakes to the skillet and cook for 3-4 minutes per side, until golden brown and crispy.
Remove the crab cakes from the skillet and serve hot, with lemon wedges on the side.
Enjoy your delicious and flavorful Crab Cakes!

Lobster Mac and Cheese

Ingredients:

1 pound elbow macaroni
4 tablespoons unsalted butter
4 tablespoons all-purpose flour
4 cups whole milk
2 cups grated cheddar cheese
1 cup grated Parmesan cheese
1/2 cup heavy cream
1/2 teaspoon garlic powder
1/4 teaspoon nutmeg
Salt and black pepper, to taste
2 cups cooked lobster meat, chopped
1/2 cup panko breadcrumbs
2 tablespoons chopped fresh parsley

Instructions:

Preheat your oven to 375°F.
Cook the elbow macaroni according to package instructions until al dente. Drain and set aside.
In a large saucepan, melt the butter over medium heat. Add the flour and whisk until smooth.
Gradually add the milk, whisking constantly, until the mixture is smooth and creamy.
Stir in the cheddar cheese, Parmesan cheese, heavy cream, garlic powder, nutmeg, salt, and black pepper, and whisk until the cheese is melted and the sauce is smooth.
Add the cooked macaroni and chopped lobster meat to the cheese sauce, and stir until well combined.
Transfer the mac and cheese to a baking dish and sprinkle with panko breadcrumbs.
Bake for 20-25 minutes, until the top is golden brown and the cheese is bubbling.
Remove the lobster mac and cheese from the oven and let it cool for a few minutes before serving.
Garnish with chopped fresh parsley and enjoy your delicious and decadent Lobster Mac and Cheese!
Note: You can also use other types of seafood such as shrimp or crab instead of lobster, or even a combination of seafood.

Air Fryer Salmon

Ingredients:

2 salmon fillets
1 tablespoon olive oil
1 teaspoon garlic powder
1 teaspoon paprika
1/2 teaspoon salt
1/4 teaspoon black pepper
Lemon wedges, for serving

Instructions:

Preheat your air fryer to 400°F.
Brush the salmon fillets with olive oil on both sides.
In a small bowl, mix together the garlic powder, paprika, salt, and black pepper.
Rub the spice mixture evenly over both sides of the salmon fillets.
Place the seasoned salmon fillets in the air fryer basket.
Cook the salmon in the air fryer for 8-10 minutes, or until it flakes easily with a fork.
Remove the salmon from the air fryer and let it cool for a few minutes.
Serve the salmon with lemon wedges on the side.
Enjoy your delicious and healthy Air Fryer Salmon, with crispy skin and moist flesh. You can also serve it with your favorite sides, such as roasted vegetables or a salad.

Connecticut-Style Lobster Roll

Ingredients:

1 pound cooked lobster meat, chopped
1/4 cup mayonnaise
2 tablespoons unsalted butter, melted
1/4 teaspoon paprika
Salt and black pepper, to taste
4 hot dog buns
2 tablespoons chopped fresh chives
Lemon wedges, for serving

Instructions:

In a large bowl, mix together the chopped lobster meat, mayonnaise, melted butter, paprika, salt, and black pepper.
Cover the bowl with plastic wrap and chill the lobster mixture in the refrigerator for at least 30 minutes.
Preheat a griddle or a large skillet over medium heat.
Brush the hot dog buns with melted butter and toast them on the griddle or skillet until golden brown.
Divide the chilled lobster mixture among the toasted hot dog buns.
Garnish the lobster rolls with chopped fresh chives.
Serve the lobster rolls immediately with lemon wedges on the side.
Enjoy your delicious Connecticut-Style Lobster Roll, with a buttery and creamy filling that highlights the sweetness of the lobster meat.

Beer Battered Fish

Ingredients:

1 pound white fish fillets (such as cod or haddock)
1 cup all-purpose flour
1 teaspoon baking powder
1/2 teaspoon salt
1/2 teaspoon black pepper
1/2 teaspoon paprika
1/2 cup beer (such as lager or pilsner)
1/4 cup milk
Vegetable oil, for frying

Instructions:

In a large bowl, whisk together the flour, baking powder, salt, black pepper, and paprika. Slowly pour in the beer and milk, whisking constantly until the batter is smooth and lump-free.
Place the fish fillets in the batter and coat them evenly, using a fork to flip and coat each piece.
In a large skillet or a deep fryer, heat the vegetable oil over medium-high heat until it reaches 375°F.
Shake off any excess batter from the fish fillets and carefully place them in the hot oil.
Fry the fish fillets for 4-5 minutes, or until they are golden brown and crispy on the outside.
Use a slotted spoon to transfer the fried fish fillets to a paper towel-lined plate to drain off any excess oil.
Repeat the frying process with the remaining fish fillets, adjusting the heat as needed to maintain the oil temperature.
Serve the beer battered fish hot, with lemon wedges and your favorite dipping sauce on the side.
Enjoy your crispy and flavorful Beer Battered Fish, with a crunchy coating that complements the juicy and flaky fish meat.

Garlic Parmesan Flounder

Ingredients:

4 flounder fillets (about 6 ounces each)
1/4 cup all-purpose flour
1/2 teaspoon garlic powder
Salt and black pepper, to taste
1/4 cup unsalted butter
2 cloves garlic, minced
1/4 cup grated Parmesan cheese
1/4 cup chopped fresh parsley

Instructions:

Preheat the oven to 375°F.
In a shallow bowl, mix together the flour, garlic powder, salt, and black pepper.
Dredge the flounder fillets in the flour mixture, shaking off any excess.
In a large skillet, melt the butter over medium heat.
Add the minced garlic and sauté for 1-2 minutes, until fragrant.
Place the flounder fillets in the skillet and cook for 2-3 minutes on each side, until lightly browned.
Transfer the flounder fillets to a baking dish.
Sprinkle the grated Parmesan cheese over the flounder fillets.
Bake the flounder fillets in the preheated oven for 10-12 minutes, or until the cheese is melted and the fish is cooked through.
Sprinkle the chopped fresh parsley over the top of the baked flounder fillets.
Serve the Garlic Parmesan Flounder hot, with lemon wedges on the side.
Enjoy your flavorful and tender Garlic Parmesan Flounder, with a rich and buttery sauce that complements the delicate fish flavor.

Shrimp Stir Fry

Ingredients:

1 lb large shrimp, peeled and deveined
2 tbsp vegetable oil, divided
1 red bell pepper, sliced
1 green bell pepper, sliced
1 onion, sliced
2 garlic cloves, minced
1 tbsp fresh ginger, minced
1 cup broccoli florets
1 cup sliced carrots
1/4 cup low sodium soy sauce
2 tbsp oyster sauce
2 tbsp honey
1 tbsp cornstarch
1/4 tsp red pepper flakes (optional)
Salt and pepper to taste
Cooked rice, for serving

Instructions:

In a small bowl, whisk together the soy sauce, oyster sauce, honey, cornstarch and red pepper flakes until combined. Set aside.
In a large skillet or wok, heat 1 tablespoon of vegetable oil over high heat. Add the shrimp and cook for 2-3 minutes on each side or until pink and opaque. Remove from the skillet and set aside.
Add the remaining tablespoon of vegetable oil to the skillet. Add the sliced peppers, onion, garlic and ginger to the skillet and cook for 3-4 minutes or until slightly softened.
Add the broccoli florets and sliced carrots to the skillet and continue cooking for an additional 3-4 minutes or until the vegetables are tender-crisp.
Return the shrimp to the skillet and pour the sauce over the top. Cook for an additional 1-2 minutes or until the sauce has thickened and the shrimp and vegetables are coated.
Serve the shrimp stir fry over cooked rice.
Enjoy your delicious and healthy Shrimp Stir Fry, packed with colorful vegetables and tasty shrimp in a flavorful sauce!

Spicy Grilled Shrimp

Ingredients:

1 pound large shrimp, peeled and deveined
1/4 cup olive oil
2 cloves garlic, minced
2 tablespoons honey
2 tablespoons fresh lime juice
1 teaspoon smoked paprika
1 teaspoon chili powder
1/4 teaspoon cayenne pepper
1/2 teaspoon salt
Lime wedges, for serving

Instructions:

Preheat grill to medium-high heat.
In a small bowl, whisk together the olive oil, garlic, honey, lime juice, smoked paprika, chili powder, cayenne pepper and salt.
Add the shrimp to the bowl and toss until well coated.
Thread the shrimp onto skewers, leaving a little space in between each shrimp.
Place the skewers on the grill and cook for 2-3 minutes per side, or until the shrimp are pink and slightly charred.
Remove the shrimp from the grill and serve with lime wedges.
Enjoy your Spicy Grilled Shrimp, perfect for a summer BBQ or quick weeknight dinner!

Pineapple Baked Salmon

Ingredients:

4 salmon fillets
1 cup fresh pineapple chunks
1/4 cup soy sauce
1/4 cup honey
2 tablespoons rice vinegar
1 tablespoon minced garlic
1 tablespoon minced ginger
1/4 teaspoon black pepper
2 tablespoons chopped green onions (optional)

Instructions:

Preheat your oven to 375°F.
In a small mixing bowl, whisk together the soy sauce, honey, rice vinegar, minced garlic, minced ginger, and black pepper.
Place the salmon fillets in a baking dish that has been lightly sprayed with cooking spray.
Pour the soy sauce mixture over the salmon fillets.
Add the fresh pineapple chunks to the baking dish, distributing them evenly around the salmon fillets.
Cover the baking dish with foil and bake in the preheated oven for 15-20 minutes, or until the salmon is cooked through and flakes easily with a fork.
Remove the foil and broil the salmon for an additional 1-2 minutes, or until the top is browned and caramelized.
Garnish with chopped green onions, if desired, and serve hot.
Enjoy your delicious Pineapple Baked Salmon!

Cheesy Shrimp And Grits

Ingredients:

For the grits:

1 cup yellow grits
4 cups water
1 cup grated cheddar cheese
Salt and pepper to taste
2 tablespoons butter

For the shrimp:

1 pound large shrimp, peeled and deveined
1 tablespoon olive oil
1 tablespoon butter
2 cloves garlic, minced
1/4 cup white wine
1/4 cup chicken broth
1/4 cup heavy cream
Salt and pepper to taste
1 tablespoon chopped parsley

Instructions:

Bring the water to a boil in a large saucepan. Add the grits and stir to combine. Reduce the heat to low and cook the grits, stirring occasionally, for about 20-25 minutes or until they are soft and creamy.
Stir in the cheddar cheese, salt, pepper, and butter until well combined. Cover the pan and keep warm.
Heat the olive oil and butter in a large skillet over medium-high heat. Add the garlic and sauté for about 30 seconds.
Add the shrimp to the skillet and cook for about 2-3 minutes on each side, or until they are pink and cooked through.
Remove the shrimp from the skillet and set aside.
Add the white wine to the skillet and stir to deglaze the pan. Add the chicken broth and heavy cream and cook for about 2-3 minutes, or until the sauce has thickened.
Return the shrimp to the skillet and stir to combine with the sauce. Cook for an additional 2-3 minutes, or until the shrimp are heated through.
Serve the shrimp and sauce over the grits. Garnish with chopped parsley.
Enjoy your delicious Cheesy Shrimp and Grits!

Greek Salmon Burger

Ingredients:

1 pound fresh salmon, skin removed and chopped into small pieces
1/4 cup crumbled feta cheese
1/4 cup chopped fresh parsley
1/4 cup chopped fresh dill
2 tablespoons chopped red onion
1 tablespoon chopped capers
1 tablespoon lemon juice
1 garlic clove, minced
Salt and pepper to taste
1 egg
1/2 cup panko breadcrumbs
4 burger buns
Toppings: sliced cucumber, tomato, red onion, and tzatziki sauce

Instructions:

In a large mixing bowl, combine the chopped salmon, feta cheese, parsley, dill, red onion, capers, lemon juice, garlic, salt, and pepper. Mix well to combine.
In a separate bowl, beat the egg and stir in the panko breadcrumbs.
Add the breadcrumb mixture to the salmon mixture and mix well to combine.
Divide the mixture into 4 equal parts and shape each portion into a patty.
Heat a large skillet over medium-high heat. Add a small amount of oil to the skillet and swirl to coat.
Place the salmon patties in the skillet and cook for about 4-5 minutes on each side, or until they are golden brown and cooked through.
Toast the burger buns in a toaster or on a grill.
Assemble the burgers with the salmon patty, sliced cucumber, tomato, red onion, and a dollop of tzatziki sauce.
Enjoy your delicious Greek Salmon Burger!

Baked Catfish

Ingredients:

4 catfish fillets
1/2 cup all-purpose flour
1/2 cup yellow cornmeal
1 teaspoon salt
1/2 teaspoon black pepper
1/2 teaspoon paprika
1/2 teaspoon garlic powder
1/2 cup buttermilk
1/4 cup vegetable oil
Lemon wedges for serving

Instructions:

Preheat your oven to 375°F.
In a shallow bowl, whisk together the flour, cornmeal, salt, black pepper, paprika, and garlic powder.
Pour the buttermilk into another shallow bowl.
Dip each catfish fillet in the buttermilk, then coat it in the flour mixture, shaking off any excess.
Heat the vegetable oil in a large skillet over medium-high heat.
Once the oil is hot, add the catfish fillets and cook for about 2-3 minutes on each side, or until they are golden brown.
Remove the catfish fillets from the skillet and place them on a baking sheet lined with parchment paper.
Bake the catfish in the preheated oven for about 10-15 minutes, or until they are cooked through and flaky.
Serve the catfish with lemon wedges on the side.
Enjoy your delicious Baked Catfish!

Greek Salmon

Ingredients:

4 salmon fillets, about 6 oz each
1/2 cup chopped kalamata olives
1/2 cup crumbled feta cheese
1/4 cup chopped fresh parsley
1/4 cup chopped fresh dill
2 tablespoons chopped red onion
2 tablespoons lemon juice
1 garlic clove, minced
Salt and pepper to taste
1/4 cup extra-virgin olive oil

Instructions:

Preheat your oven to 400°F.
In a small bowl, mix together the chopped olives, feta cheese, parsley, dill, red onion, lemon juice, garlic, salt, and pepper.
Spread the olive mixture over the salmon fillets, making sure to cover them completely.
Drizzle the olive oil over the salmon.
Place the salmon on a baking sheet lined with parchment paper.
Bake the salmon in the preheated oven for about 12-15 minutes, or until it is cooked through and flaky.
Serve the salmon with your favorite sides, such as roasted vegetables, rice, or a salad.
Enjoy your delicious Greek-style salmon!

Pan-Fried Tilapia

Ingredients:

4 tilapia fillets
1/2 cup all-purpose flour
1/2 teaspoon garlic powder
1/2 teaspoon paprika
1/2 teaspoon salt
1/4 teaspoon black pepper
2 tablespoons vegetable oil
Lemon wedges for serving

Instructions:

Rinse the tilapia fillets under cold water and pat them dry with paper towels.
In a shallow bowl, whisk together the flour, garlic powder, paprika, salt, and black pepper.
Dip each tilapia fillet in the flour mixture, shaking off any excess.
Heat the vegetable oil in a large skillet over medium-high heat.
Once the oil is hot, add the tilapia fillets and cook for about 2-3 minutes on each side, or until they are golden brown and crispy.
Remove the tilapia fillets from the skillet and place them on a paper towel-lined plate to drain any excess oil.
Serve the tilapia with lemon wedges on the side.
Enjoy your delicious Pan-Fried Tilapia!

Jalapeño Citrus Salmon

Ingredients:

4 salmon fillets, about 6 oz each
1 jalapeño pepper, seeded and finely chopped
1/4 cup orange juice
2 tablespoons lime juice
2 tablespoons honey
2 garlic cloves, minced
1 teaspoon ground cumin
1/2 teaspoon paprika
Salt and pepper to taste
2 tablespoons vegetable oil
Orange and lime wedges for serving

Instructions:

Preheat your oven to 400°F.
In a small bowl, whisk together the jalapeño pepper, orange juice, lime juice, honey, garlic, cumin, paprika, salt, and pepper.
Place the salmon fillets in a baking dish and pour the jalapeño citrus mixture over them, making sure to coat them well.
Heat the vegetable oil in a large skillet over medium-high heat.
Once the oil is hot, add the salmon fillets and cook for about 2-3 minutes on each side, or until they are browned.
Transfer the salmon fillets to the oven and bake for about 8-10 minutes, or until they are cooked through and flaky.
Serve the salmon with orange and lime wedges on the side.
Enjoy your delicious Jalapeño Citrus Salmon!

Baked Scallops

Ingredients:

1 lb fresh sea scallops
4 tablespoons unsalted butter, melted
1/4 cup dry white wine
1/4 cup breadcrumbs
1/4 cup grated Parmesan cheese
1 tablespoon minced fresh parsley
1 garlic clove, minced
Salt and pepper to taste
Lemon wedges for serving

Instructions:

Preheat your oven to 425°F.

Rinse the sea scallops under cold water and pat them dry with paper towels.

In a small bowl, mix together the melted butter, white wine, breadcrumbs, Parmesan cheese, parsley, garlic, salt, and pepper.

Place the scallops in a baking dish and pour the breadcrumb mixture over them, making sure to coat them well.

Bake the scallops in the preheated oven for about 10-12 minutes, or until they are cooked through and golden brown on top.

Serve the scallops with lemon wedges on the side.

Enjoy your delicious Baked Scallops!

Lobster Bisque

Ingredients:

2 lobsters (about 2 pounds each)
6 cups of water
2 tablespoons of olive oil
1 onion, chopped
1 carrot, chopped
1 celery stalk, chopped
1 garlic clove, minced
1 bay leaf
1/4 teaspoon of thyme
1/4 cup of brandy
3 tablespoons of tomato paste
4 cups of fish or chicken broth
1 cup of heavy cream
Salt and pepper to taste
Chopped fresh parsley for garnish

Instructions:

Fill a large pot with 6 cups of water and bring it to a boil over high heat. Add the lobsters and cook them for about 8-10 minutes, until they turn red and the shells are firm. Remove the lobsters from the pot and let them cool.

Once the lobsters are cool enough to handle, remove the meat from the shells and chop it into small pieces. Set aside the lobster meat and keep the shells.

In a large pot or Dutch oven, heat the olive oil over medium-high heat. Add the onion, carrot, celery, garlic, bay leaf, and thyme. Cook for about 10 minutes, until the vegetables are soft and fragrant.

Add the brandy to the pot and cook for 2-3 minutes, until it has evaporated. Stir in the tomato paste and cook for another minute.

Add the fish or chicken broth to the pot and stir to combine. Add the lobster shells to the pot and bring the mixture to a simmer. Cook for about 30 minutes, until the shells have infused the broth with flavor.

Remove the lobster shells from the pot and discard them. Use an immersion blender or transfer the soup to a blender and puree until smooth.

Return the soup to the pot and add the chopped lobster meat. Simmer for 5-10 minutes, until the lobster meat is heated through. Stir in the heavy cream and cook for an additional 2-3 minutes.

Season the bisque with salt and pepper to taste. Ladle the soup into bowls and garnish with chopped fresh parsley.

Enjoy your delicious Lobster Bisque!

Shrimp Po' Boy

Ingredients:

1 pound of large shrimp, peeled and deveined
1/2 cup of cornmeal
1/2 cup of all-purpose flour
1 teaspoon of garlic powder
1 teaspoon of paprika
1/2 teaspoon of cayenne pepper
Salt and pepper to taste
Vegetable oil for frying
2 French baguettes, cut in half lengthwise
Lettuce leaves
Sliced tomato
Sliced red onion
Pickles (optional)
Remoulade sauce (see recipe below)

Instructions:
In a shallow bowl, mix together the cornmeal, flour, garlic powder, paprika, cayenne pepper, salt, and pepper.
Heat about 1/2 inch of vegetable oil in a large skillet over medium-high heat.
Coat the shrimp in the cornmeal mixture, shaking off any excess. Fry the shrimp in the hot oil until they are golden brown and cooked through, about 2-3 minutes per side. Remove the shrimp from the oil and place them on a paper towel-lined plate to drain.

To make the remoulade sauce, mix together the mayonnaise, mustard, capers, parsley, green onions, garlic, paprika, Worcestershire sauce, salt, and pepper in a small bowl.
To assemble the Po' Boys, spread the remoulade sauce on the bottom half of each baguette. Top with lettuce, sliced tomato, red onion, pickles (if using), and fried shrimp. Top with the other half of the baguette and serve immediately.
Enjoy your delicious Shrimp Po' Boy!

Garlicky Lemon Mahi Mahi

Ingredients:

4 Mahi Mahi fillets
Salt and pepper to taste
1/4 cup of all-purpose flour
2 tablespoons of olive oil
4 garlic cloves, minced
1/2 cup of chicken or vegetable broth
2 tablespoons of fresh lemon juice
1 tablespoon of butter
1 tablespoon of chopped fresh parsley

Instructions:

Season the Mahi Mahi fillets with salt and pepper, and dredge them in flour to coat.
Heat the olive oil in a large skillet over medium-high heat. Add the Mahi Mahi fillets to the skillet and cook for about 4-5 minutes per side, until they are golden brown and cooked through. Remove the fillets from the skillet and keep them warm.
Add the minced garlic to the skillet and cook for about 1 minute, until fragrant. Pour the chicken or vegetable broth into the skillet, stirring to scrape up any browned bits from the bottom of the pan. Bring the mixture to a simmer and cook for about 2-3 minutes, until the liquid has reduced by half.
Stir in the lemon juice and butter, and cook for another minute or two, until the butter has melted and the sauce has thickened slightly.
Spoon the sauce over the Mahi Mahi fillets and sprinkle with chopped parsley.
Serve the Garlicky Lemon Mahi Mahi immediately, accompanied by your favorite side dishes.
Enjoy your delicious Garlicky Lemon Mahi Mahi!

Creamed Spinach Stuffed Salmon

Ingredients:

4 salmon fillets, skin removed
Salt and pepper to taste
1 tablespoon of olive oil
1 onion, diced
2 garlic cloves, minced
10 ounces of frozen chopped spinach, thawed and drained
4 ounces of cream cheese, softened
1/4 cup of grated Parmesan cheese
1/4 cup of heavy cream
1/4 teaspoon of nutmeg

Instructions:

Preheat the oven to 375°F.
Season the salmon fillets with salt and pepper. Set aside.
In a large skillet, heat the olive oil over medium heat. Add the onion and garlic and cook until softened, about 5-7 minutes.
Add the spinach to the skillet and cook for another 2-3 minutes, until heated through.
Add the cream cheese, Parmesan cheese, heavy cream, and nutmeg to the skillet. Stir to combine, and cook until the cheese is melted and the mixture is heated through.
Lay the salmon fillets out on a work surface. Using a sharp knife, make a lengthwise slit in the center of each fillet, taking care not to cut all the way through.
Stuff the creamed spinach mixture into the slit in each fillet, using a spoon to distribute it evenly.
Place the stuffed salmon fillets in a baking dish and bake for 15-20 minutes, until the salmon is cooked through and the filling is hot and bubbly.
Serve the Creamed Spinach Stuffed Salmon immediately, garnished with fresh herbs or lemon wedges if desired.
Enjoy your delicious Creamed Spinach Stuffed Salmon!
ChatGPT Mar 14 Version. Free Research Preview. Our goal is to make AI systems more natural and safe to interact with. Your feedback will help us improve.

Shrimp Alfredo

Ingredients:

1 pound of shrimp, peeled and deveined
Salt and pepper to taste
8 ounces of fettuccine pasta
1/4 cup of unsalted butter
3 garlic cloves, minced
1 cup of heavy cream
1/2 cup of grated Parmesan cheese
1/4 teaspoon of nutmeg
1/4 cup of chopped fresh parsley

Instructions:

Bring a large pot of salted water to a boil. Add the fettuccine pasta and cook according to package directions until al dente. Drain the pasta and set it aside. Meanwhile, season the shrimp with salt and pepper. In a large skillet, melt the butter over medium heat. Add the shrimp to the skillet and cook for 2-3 minutes per side, until pink and cooked through. Remove the shrimp from the skillet and set them aside.
Add the minced garlic to the skillet and cook for 1-2 minutes, until fragrant.
Pour the heavy cream into the skillet, stirring to scrape up any browned bits from the bottom of the pan. Bring the mixture to a simmer and cook for about 5 minutes, until the cream has thickened slightly.
Stir in the grated Parmesan cheese and nutmeg, and cook for another 1-2 minutes, until the cheese has melted and the sauce is smooth.
Return the cooked shrimp to the skillet and stir to coat them in the sauce.
Add the cooked fettuccine pasta to the skillet, tossing to coat it in the sauce.
Sprinkle chopped parsley over the Shrimp Alfredo and serve immediately.
Enjoy your delicious Shrimp Alfredo!

Honey Walnut Shrimp

Ingredients:

1 pound of large shrimp, peeled and deveined
Salt and pepper to taste
1/2 cup of cornstarch
1/4 cup of mayonnaise
1/4 cup of honey
2 tablespoons of sweetened condensed milk
1/2 cup of walnuts, roughly chopped
Vegetable oil for frying

Instructions:

Season the shrimp with salt and pepper. In a shallow bowl, toss the shrimp with cornstarch to coat.
Heat the vegetable oil in a deep skillet over medium-high heat. Once hot, fry the coated shrimp in batches until they are golden brown and crispy, about 2-3 minutes per batch. Remove the fried shrimp with a slotted spoon and drain on paper towels.
In a small saucepan, combine the mayonnaise, honey, and sweetened condensed milk. Cook over low heat, stirring constantly, until the mixture is smooth and warmed through.
Add the chopped walnuts to the saucepan, stirring to coat them in the sauce.
Pour the sauce over the fried shrimp, tossing to coat them evenly.
Serve the Honey Walnut Shrimp immediately, garnished with additional chopped walnuts and chopped scallions if desired.
Enjoy your delicious Honey Walnut Shrimp!

Spaghetti alla Frutti di Mare

Ingredients:

1 pound of spaghetti
1/4 cup of olive oil
3 garlic cloves, minced
1/2 teaspoon of red pepper flakes
1/2 cup of white wine
1 pound of mixed seafood (such as mussels, clams, shrimp, and calamari), cleaned and scrubbed
1 can (14 ounces) of diced tomatoes
Salt and pepper to taste
1/4 cup of chopped fresh parsley
Lemon wedges for serving

Instructions:

Cook the spaghetti in a large pot of salted boiling water according to package directions until al dente. Drain the spaghetti and set it aside.
In a large skillet, heat the olive oil over medium heat. Add the garlic and red pepper flakes and cook for 1-2 minutes, until fragrant.
Add the white wine to the skillet, stirring to scrape up any browned bits from the bottom of the pan. Bring the wine to a simmer and cook for 1-2 minutes, until it has reduced slightly.
Add the mixed seafood to the skillet, stirring to coat it in the wine mixture. Cover the skillet and cook for 5-7 minutes, until the seafood is cooked through and the shells have opened.
Add the diced tomatoes to the skillet, stirring to combine. Cook for another 1-2 minutes, until the tomatoes are heated through.
Season the seafood sauce with salt and pepper to taste.
Add the cooked spaghetti to the skillet, tossing to coat it in the seafood sauce.
Sprinkle chopped fresh parsley over the Spaghetti alla Frutti di Mare and serve immediately, with lemon wedges on the side.
Enjoy your delicious Spaghetti alla Frutti di Mare!

Seafood Jambalaya

Ingredients:

1 pound of shrimp, peeled and deveined
1 pound of scallops
1 pound of mussels, scrubbed and debearded
1/2 pound of Andouille sausage, sliced
1 onion, diced
1 green bell pepper, diced
3 celery stalks, diced
3 garlic cloves, minced
1 can (14.5 ounces) of diced tomatoes
1 teaspoon of dried thyme
1 teaspoon of dried oregano
1 teaspoon of paprika
1 teaspoon of cayenne pepper
1 teaspoon of salt
1/2 teaspoon of black pepper
1 bay leaf
2 cups of chicken broth
2 cups of long-grain white rice
3 tablespoons of chopped fresh parsley

Instructions:

Heat a large Dutch oven over medium-high heat. Add the sliced Andouille sausage and cook for 5-7 minutes, until browned. Remove the sausage from the Dutch oven and set it aside.
Add the diced onion, green bell pepper, and celery to the Dutch oven. Cook for 5-7 minutes, until the vegetables are softened.
Add the minced garlic to the Dutch oven and cook for 1-2 minutes, until fragrant.
Add the diced tomatoes, dried thyme, dried oregano, paprika, cayenne pepper, salt, black pepper, and bay leaf to the Dutch oven, stirring to combine.
Pour the chicken broth into the Dutch oven, stirring to combine. Bring the mixture to a simmer.
Add the uncooked rice to the Dutch oven, stirring to combine. Cover the Dutch oven with a lid and simmer for 20-25 minutes, until the rice is cooked through and the liquid has been absorbed.
Add the shrimp, scallops, mussels, and cooked Andouille sausage to the Dutch oven, stirring to combine. Cover the Dutch oven with a lid and cook for another 5-7 minutes, until the seafood is cooked through and the mussels have opened.
Discard any mussels that did not open. Sprinkle chopped fresh parsley over the Seafood Jambalaya and serve hot.
Enjoy your delicious Seafood Jambalaya!

Tuscan Butter Salmon

Ingredients:

4 salmon fillets, skin-on
Salt and black pepper to taste
1 tablespoon of olive oil
1/4 cup of unsalted butter, softened
3 garlic cloves, minced
1/4 cup of sun-dried tomatoes, chopped
1/4 cup of freshly grated Parmesan cheese
1/4 cup of fresh basil leaves, chopped
1/4 cup of heavy cream

Instructions:

Preheat your oven to 375°F (190°C).
Season the salmon fillets with salt and black pepper to taste.
Heat the olive oil in a large oven-safe skillet over medium-high heat.
Add the salmon fillets, skin-side down, to the skillet. Cook for 2-3 minutes, until the skin is crispy and golden brown.
Flip the salmon fillets and transfer the skillet to the preheated oven. Bake for 8-10 minutes, until the salmon is cooked through.
In a mixing bowl, combine the softened butter, minced garlic, chopped sun-dried tomatoes, freshly grated Parmesan cheese, chopped basil leaves, and heavy cream.
Microwave the butter mixture for 30 seconds, stirring every 10 seconds, until the butter is melted and the ingredients are well combined.
Remove the salmon from the oven and pour the Tuscan butter sauce over the salmon fillets.
Return the skillet to the oven and broil for 1-2 minutes, until the Tuscan butter sauce is bubbly and golden brown.
Serve the Tuscan Butter Salmon hot, garnished with additional chopped fresh basil leaves, if desired.
Enjoy your delicious Tuscan Butter Salmon!

Shrimp Ceviche

Ingredients:

1 pound of cooked shrimp, peeled and deveined
1/2 cup of freshly squeezed lime juice
1/4 cup of freshly squeezed orange juice
1/2 cup of diced tomato
1/2 cup of diced cucumber
1/2 cup of diced red onion
1 jalapeño pepper, seeded and minced
1/4 cup of chopped cilantro
Salt and black pepper to taste
Tortilla chips or crackers, for serving

Instructions:

Cut the cooked shrimp into bite-sized pieces and place them in a large mixing bowl.
Pour the freshly squeezed lime juice and orange juice over the shrimp, stirring to combine. Make sure that all the shrimp is coated in the citrus juice.
Cover the mixing bowl with plastic wrap and refrigerate for 30 minutes to 1 hour, until the shrimp is opaque and no longer translucent.
Remove the mixing bowl from the refrigerator and add the diced tomato, diced cucumber, diced red onion, minced jalapeño pepper, and chopped cilantro. Stir to combine.
Season the Shrimp Ceviche with salt and black pepper to taste.
Serve the Shrimp Ceviche cold, with tortilla chips or crackers for dipping.
Enjoy your delicious Shrimp Ceviche!

Blackened Salmon Tacos

Ingredients:

4 salmon fillets, skin-off
2 tablespoons of blackened seasoning
Salt and black pepper to taste
8 corn tortillas
1 avocado, sliced
1/2 cup of diced tomato
1/2 cup of diced red onion
1/4 cup of chopped cilantro
1 lime, cut into wedges
Sour cream and hot sauce, for serving

Instructions:

Preheat your grill or grill pan to medium-high heat.
Season the salmon fillets with blackened seasoning, salt, and black pepper to taste.
Grill the salmon fillets for 3-4 minutes per side, until they are cooked through and slightly charred on the outside.
Remove the salmon from the grill and let it rest for a few minutes.
Heat the corn tortillas on the grill or grill pan for 1-2 minutes per side, until they are warm and slightly charred.
Flake the salmon into bite-sized pieces.
Assemble the tacos by placing a few pieces of salmon onto each warm tortilla. Top with sliced avocado, diced tomato, diced red onion, chopped cilantro, and a squeeze of lime juice.
Serve the Blackened Salmon Tacos with sour cream and hot sauce on the side.
Enjoy your delicious Blackened Salmon Tacos!

Shrimp Scampi Flatbread

Ingredients:

1 flatbread or naan bread
1/4 cup of unsalted butter
3 garlic cloves, minced
1/2 pound of cooked and peeled shrimp
1/4 cup of white wine
Juice of 1/2 lemon
Salt and black pepper to taste
1/4 cup of freshly grated Parmesan cheese
1/4 cup of chopped fresh parsley
Red pepper flakes, for garnish

Instructions:

Preheat your oven to 425°F (218°C).
Melt the unsalted butter in a skillet over medium heat.
Add the minced garlic to the skillet and sauté for 1-2 minutes, until fragrant.
Add the cooked and peeled shrimp to the skillet and cook for 2-3 minutes, until they are heated through.
Pour the white wine and lemon juice into the skillet, stirring to combine. Season the Shrimp Scampi mixture with salt and black pepper to taste.
Spread the Shrimp Scampi mixture onto the flatbread or naan bread.
Sprinkle the freshly grated Parmesan cheese over the Shrimp Scampi mixture.
Bake the Shrimp Scampi Flatbread in the preheated oven for 8-10 minutes, until the cheese is melted and the flatbread is crispy.
Remove the Shrimp Scampi Flatbread from the oven and sprinkle with chopped fresh parsley and red pepper flakes, if desired.
Cut the Shrimp Scampi Flatbread into slices and serve hot.
Enjoy your delicious Shrimp Scampi Flatbread!

Mussels with Tomatoes and Garlic

Ingredients:

2 pounds of mussels, scrubbed and debearded
1 tablespoon of olive oil
4 garlic cloves, minced
1/4 teaspoon of red pepper flakes
1/2 cup of dry white wine
1 cup of diced tomatoes
1/4 cup of chopped fresh parsley
Salt and black pepper to taste
Crusty bread, for serving

Instructions:

Heat the olive oil in a large pot over medium heat.
Add the minced garlic and red pepper flakes to the pot and sauté for 1-2 minutes, until fragrant.
Pour the dry white wine into the pot and bring it to a simmer.
Add the scrubbed and debearded mussels to the pot, stirring to coat them in the garlic and wine mixture.
Cover the pot and cook for 5-7 minutes, until the mussels have opened.
Use a slotted spoon to remove the cooked mussels from the pot and set them aside in a bowl, discarding any unopened mussels.
Add the diced tomatoes to the pot and stir to combine.
Cook the tomato mixture for 3-4 minutes, until the sauce has thickened slightly.
Season the tomato mixture with salt and black pepper to taste.
Pour the tomato mixture over the cooked mussels in the bowl.
Sprinkle chopped fresh parsley over the mussels and tomato sauce.
Serve the Mussels with Tomatoes and Garlic hot, with crusty bread for dipping in the flavorful broth.
Enjoy your delicious Mussels with Tomatoes and Garlic!

Shrimp Fried Rice

Ingredients:

3 cups of cooked white rice
1 pound of medium-sized shrimp, peeled and deveined
3 tablespoons of vegetable oil
3 eggs, lightly beaten
1 cup of frozen mixed vegetables (carrots, peas, corn)
2 garlic cloves, minced
1/2 cup of diced onion
1 tablespoon of soy sauce
1 tablespoon of oyster sauce
Salt and black pepper to taste
Green onions, thinly sliced, for garnish

Instructions:

Heat 1 tablespoon of vegetable oil in a wok or large skillet over medium-high heat.

Add the beaten eggs to the wok and scramble them until fully cooked. Remove the eggs from the wok and set them aside in a bowl.
Heat the remaining 2 tablespoons of vegetable oil in the wok.
Add the minced garlic and diced onion to the wok and sauté for 2-3 minutes, until fragrant and softened.
Add the peeled and deveined shrimp to the wok and cook for 2-3 minutes, until they turn pink and are cooked through.
Add the frozen mixed vegetables to the wok and cook for an additional 2-3 minutes, until they are heated through.
Add the cooked white rice to the wok and stir to combine with the shrimp and vegetable mixture.
Pour the soy sauce and oyster sauce over the rice mixture, stirring to coat everything evenly.
Season the Shrimp Fried Rice with salt and black pepper to taste.
Add the scrambled eggs back to the wok, stirring to distribute them throughout the rice mixture.
Cook for an additional 2-3 minutes, until everything is heated through.
Serve the Shrimp Fried Rice hot, garnished with thinly sliced green onions.
Enjoy your delicious Shrimp Fried Rice!

New England Clam Chowder

Ingredients:

6 slices of bacon, chopped
1 onion, diced
2 celery stalks, diced
2 cloves of garlic, minced
2 tablespoons of all-purpose flour
4 cups of chicken or vegetable broth
4 cups of diced potatoes
3 cups of chopped fresh clams (or 3 cans of chopped clams)
2 cups of heavy cream
2 bay leaves
Salt and black pepper to taste
Oyster crackers, for serving

Instructions:

In a large pot or Dutch oven, cook the chopped bacon over medium heat until crispy.
Remove the cooked bacon from the pot and set it aside in a bowl.
Add the diced onion and celery to the bacon fat in the pot and sauté for 5-7 minutes, until softened.
Add the minced garlic to the pot and sauté for an additional 1-2 minutes, until fragrant.
Sprinkle the all-purpose flour over the sautéed vegetables, stirring to combine.
Slowly pour the chicken or vegetable broth into the pot, whisking continuously to prevent lumps from forming.
Add the diced potatoes and bay leaves to the pot.
Bring the mixture to a boil, then reduce the heat and simmer for 15-20 minutes, until the potatoes are tender.
Add the chopped fresh clams or canned clams and their juice to the pot.
Pour in the heavy cream and stir to combine.
Season the New England Clam Chowder with salt and black pepper to taste.
Simmer the chowder for an additional 10-15 minutes, until the flavors have melded together.
Serve the New England Clam Chowder hot, garnished with the reserved crispy bacon and oyster crackers.
Enjoy your delicious New England Clam Chowder!

Grilled Tilapia

Ingredients:

4 Tilapia fillets
1 tablespoon of olive oil
Salt and pepper to taste
1 teaspoon of garlic powder
1 teaspoon of paprika
1/2 teaspoon of cumin
1/2 teaspoon of dried oregano
1/4 teaspoon of cayenne pepper (optional)
Lemon wedges (optional)

Instructions:

Preheat the grill to medium-high heat.
In a small bowl, mix the olive oil, garlic powder, paprika, cumin, oregano, and cayenne pepper (if using).
Season both sides of the Tilapia fillets with salt and pepper.
Brush the spice mixture on both sides of the Tilapia fillets.
Place the Tilapia fillets on the grill and cook for 3-4 minutes on each side, or until the fish is cooked through and flakes easily with a fork.
Remove from the grill and serve with lemon wedges (if using).

Enjoy your delicious Grilled Tilapia!

Shrimp Creole

Ingredients:

1 lb. medium shrimp, peeled and deveined
2 tablespoons of vegetable oil
1 onion, diced
1 green bell pepper, diced
2 celery stalks, diced
2 cloves of garlic, minced
1 can (14.5 oz) of diced tomatoes
1 can (8 oz) of tomato sauce
1 tablespoon of Worcestershire sauce
1 tablespoon of hot sauce
1 tablespoon of paprika
1/2 teaspoon of dried thyme
1/2 teaspoon of dried oregano
Salt and black pepper to taste
Cooked white rice, for serving
Chopped fresh parsley for garnish

Instructions:

Heat the oil in a large skillet over medium-high heat. Add the onion, bell pepper, and celery and cook until softened, about 5 minutes. Add the garlic and cook for an additional minute.
Stir in the diced tomatoes, tomato sauce, Worcestershire sauce, hot sauce, paprika, thyme, and oregano. Season with salt and black pepper to taste.
Bring the mixture to a simmer and let it cook for about 10-15 minutes until the sauce thickens.
Add the shrimp and cook for 3-4 minutes or until the shrimp are cooked through and turn pink.
Serve over cooked white rice and garnish with chopped parsley.
Enjoy your delicious Shrimp Creole!

Spaghetti with Clams and Garlic

Ingredients:

1 lb spaghetti
3 tablespoons of olive oil
4 cloves of garlic, minced
1/2 teaspoon of red pepper flakes (optional)
1/2 cup of white wine
2 cans (6.5 oz each) of minced clams, drained
Salt and black pepper to taste
Chopped fresh parsley for garnish

Instructions:

Cook the spaghetti according to the package instructions until al dente.
While the spaghetti is cooking, heat the olive oil in a large skillet over medium heat. Add the garlic and red pepper flakes (if using) and cook until fragrant, about 1-2 minutes.
Add the white wine and bring it to a simmer. Cook for about 2-3 minutes or until the wine has reduced by half.
Add the drained clams and cook for an additional 2-3 minutes, until the clams are heated through.
Season the sauce with salt and black pepper to taste.
Drain the cooked spaghetti and add it to the skillet with the clam sauce. Toss the spaghetti with the sauce until it is well coated.
Serve the spaghetti with chopped fresh parsley for garnish.
Enjoy your delicious Spaghetti with Clams and Garlic!

Maine-Style Lobster Rolls

Ingredients:

1 lb cooked lobster meat, chopped
1/4 cup of mayonnaise
1 tablespoon of lemon juice
Salt and black pepper to taste
4 hot dog buns
2 tablespoons of butter, melted
Chopped fresh parsley for garnish

Instructions:

In a bowl, mix together the chopped lobster meat, mayonnaise, and lemon juice.
Season the mixture with salt and black pepper to taste.
Preheat a skillet over medium heat.
Brush the melted butter on the outside of the hot dog buns.
Toast the buns in the skillet until they are lightly golden brown.
Fill each bun with the lobster mixture.
Garnish with chopped fresh parsley.

Enjoy your delicious Maine-Style Lobster Rolls!

Lobster BLTs on Potato Rolls

Ingredients:

1 lb cooked lobster meat, chopped
1/2 cup of mayonnaise
2 tablespoons of lemon juice
Salt and black pepper to taste
8 slices of bacon, cooked until crispy
4 large potato rolls
Lettuce leaves
Sliced tomatoes

Instructions:

In a bowl, mix together the chopped lobster meat, mayonnaise, and lemon juice.
Season the mixture with salt and black pepper to taste.
Slice the potato rolls in half horizontally.
Place a lettuce leaf and a few slices of tomato on the bottom half of each roll.
Divide the lobster mixture among the rolls, spreading it evenly on top of the lettuce and tomato.
Top each roll with two slices of bacon and the top half of the roll.
Serve immediately.

Enjoy your delicious Lobster BLTs on Potato Rolls!

Mussels with Harissa and Basil

Ingredients:

2 lbs fresh mussels, scrubbed and debearded
2 tablespoons of olive oil
2 tablespoons of butter
1 onion, chopped
2 garlic cloves, minced
2 teaspoons of harissa paste
1 cup of white wine
1/2 cup of chicken or vegetable broth
Salt and black pepper to taste
1/4 cup of fresh basil leaves, chopped
Crusty bread, for serving

Instructions:

In a large pot or Dutch oven, heat the olive oil and butter over medium heat.
Add the chopped onion and garlic and cook until the onion is translucent, about 5 minutes.
Stir in the harissa paste and cook for an additional minute.
Pour in the white wine and chicken or vegetable broth and bring to a simmer.
Add the mussels to the pot and cover with a tight-fitting lid. Cook for 5-7 minutes, or until the mussels have opened.
Remove any mussels that do not open.
Season the broth with salt and black pepper to taste.
Stir in the chopped basil.
Serve the mussels and broth in bowls with crusty bread for dipping.

Enjoy your delicious Mussels with Harissa and Basil!

I want to take a moment to express my heartfelt gratitude for your recent purchase of my recipe book. As a passionate food lover, nothing makes me happier than sharing my favorite recipes with others. Your decision to invest in my book not only supports my dream, but also shows your commitment to expanding your culinary horizons.

I sincerely hope that the recipes in the book will inspire you to try new things and add some excitement to your meals.

Thank you again for your support and for being a part of this journey with me. I hope my book will bring you many happy and delicious moments in the kitchen.

www.ingramcontent.com/pod-product-compliance
Lightning Source LLC
Chambersburg PA
CBHW042036100526
44587CB00030B/4455